Never Too Old to Live

Never Too Old to Live

Never Too Late to Change

A Self-Health Book™

Jerry Rhoads

To order additional copies of this book, contact:
Xlibris Corporation
1-888-795-4274
www.Xlibris.com
Orders@Xlibris.com
107488

CONTENTS

We have so long failed to understand the wonderful power of thought for it is taught by every religion and philosophy in the history of the world. Paul, when in captivity and chained to a Roman soldier gave to the world this message:

> *Finally, brethren whatsoever things are true, whatsoever things are honest, whatsoever things are just, whatsoever things are pure, whatsoever things are lovely and of good report; if there be any virtue and there be any praise, think on these things.*

Most of us have overlooked the meaning of that verse. We have been so busy admiring its beauty of diction that we failed to place emphasis on the word think. If everybody followed Paul's injunction and thought only in terms of truth, honesty, justice, purity and loveliness, this world would be transformed from a planet of confusion, sickness and poverty into one of radiant health, happiness, and prosperity.

Quoted from Venice Bloodworth's wonderful book The Key to Yourself.

STOP
*SAYING YOU'RE
"TOO OLD TO LIVE"
THE LIFE OF YOUR
DREAMS*

START BELIEVING YOU'RE "NEVER TOO OLD TO LIVE"
A SELF-HEALTH BOOK ™

Definition: old . . . past its time, out of stock, rickety, weak, no longer relevant, retired, over the hill, decrypted, out of touch, past its prime.

How many of us are willing to refer to ourselves as old? _____10%_____5%_____1% or _____0%. Just check mark the category you're in . . . if you believe you're old you are old at any age. My point of this exercise is to define old as someone else not me. Of course that is just a mental exercise.

Let's try another definition: old, little or no exercise, poor eating habits, stinkin' thinkin', hateful attitude, cynical, low esteem, unworthy, unemployed, divorced, sickly, dull, boring, unhappy, dead before death.

My point here is obvious . . . if you are any of these conscious states you are aging too fast and are not far from disease, chemical use, poverty, criminal behavior, lack of friends, spouses, children, relationships . . . you're old at any age.

Is this speculation or fact? Is this just my opinion?

Look at the statistics:

- Divorces over 50% of those who marry get divorced
- Drug use over 75% of those depressed actively use drugs, alcohol or substances to drop out
- Life expectancy
  ° Females 80
  ° Males 70
- Retirement
  ° Females 62
  ° Males 65

Signs and symptoms of true youth:

- Happy
- Healthy
- Prosperous
- Faithful
- Positive
- Goal Seeking

What's your emotional and mental age?

If you are emotionally old . . . the sun is setting on your future. No hope, no job, no marriage, no relationships, no life . . . If you are mentally old, the moon has eclipsed on your past, no dreams fulfilled, no love gained, no successful events, no joyful memories, no happy bed time stories, no value of life as you know it.

This state of affairs can and must be reversed for you to age naturally and happy and healthy, and prosperous. Many will just accept unhappiness as happenstance that one must endure, while in waiting for happenstance to change. Guess what, it does not happen if your stance is on blaming others or just good ole circumstance. Good luck on making that work.

The cure is, as always, in your head . . . you either think young or feel old . . . why not feel young and forget thinkin' old.

Rhonda Byrne in her timely and best selling guide to happiness "The Secret", states: "life isn't happening to you, life is responding to you. Life is your call. You are the creator of your life. You decide what your life will be. " Through the Universal Law of Attraction, you attract your own results through your own thoughts and actions.

Depok Chopra in his "7 Spiritual Laws of Success" establishes: that thinking, doing and finding happiness is a mental process from Karma (giving) to Dharma (finding your true talent and place in the Universe.

Dr. Venice Bloodworth in her book "The Key to Yourself" states: that an affirmation of "I am happy, healthy and prosperous" is not just words it is the retraining of the subconscious to be positive which is a principle of Universal law that puts aside the negative as being a result of not following Universal law.

Earle Nightengale in his teachings stated that "what you can conceive and believe you will achieve".

The rest of "Never Too Old to Live" will fill in some blanks based on a number of human examples.

Think about this before you think about yourself:

- 10% of the people lead the 90%
- 90% of the people would like to lead but don't
- Why not?
  - Fear of the unknown
  - Not goal driven
  - Not prepared
  - Not risk takers
- What does this have to do with aging?
  - Fear causes stress that causes premature aging
  - Fear, stress and depression cause loss of sexuality
  - Goals are set but not pursued causing disappointment, stress and aging
  - Little or no preparation causes failure, stress and aging
  - Allowing Ego to prevail causes selfishness, stress and aging

    °   Hiding behind excuses due to risk of rejection causes, hesitancy, stress and aging

Eliminate the above negatives and live for a stress free ageless life.

Being stress free is a process:

- Decide that you can overcome your fears . . . state them then confront them
- Set simple goals that can be accomplished then savor more ambitious successes
- Find a place for your self satisfaction in giving to others and loving your present life and mate
- Prepare each with a healthy agenda (age-nda means a health plan for the day including food, exercise, thoughts of love, acts of kindness)
- Stick your neck out for causes you stand for then take action to help others find their agenda
- What you reach is what you teach others. What you miss is what you are missing. Teach those you meet what they are missing.

The results are guaranteed:

1. You will be happier
2. You will be healthier
3. You will feel younger
4. You will not age due to stress

Sounds good but what can I do to get there? GET RID OF THE STRESS USING THIS SELF-HEALTH BOOK!

> My wife (pictured with me on the cover) and her Aunt Edith are an example of laughter extending life's journey . . . Aunt Edith died at the age of 109 after being married 80 years to Uncle Ernie who was 101 when he moved on to the next continuum. Shari's mom Dorotha C. White was another of life's miracles . . . she was neglected and abused in the nursing home system and died prematurely at the age of 92, well on her way to 100 if circumstances had not intervened.

Shari's sister died of cancer at the age of 66 and her father had the same fate at the age of 67 of the same disease . . . irony never ceases in our Life stories. Shari and I are now in our seventies and convinced we can live to over 100 . . . our marriage of 52 years, 4 wonderful children and 12 gorgeous grandchildren later are hard to fathom but very heart warming. Will this book prevent cancer? Heck no! But it can reduce stress that causes cancer.

Is this approach right for you . . . you need to answer that for your own self satisfaction . . . we only know what works for us. But we do know that life is a gift that comes from the feeling of doing good, making a difference in others' lives virtually every way and every day . . . a life of feeling love for life itself. You are never too old to live this way. Travel the journey with love not hate and let age be the result of, not the reason for, changing your thinking.

But realize that change is not the reason for the self-health diet . . . it is the result. In my life the challenges have been both mental and physical. I was called "Tiny" in Junior High and High School due to being short but the coaches felt I had the most determination of all the better athletes. Never the star but always working for that goal . . . sports were my inspiration then and now . . . I love the competition but more so the accomplishments of being mentally and physically active. Then mental fulfillment is connected to wanting to excel at something. Since none of us are born excellent, smart, sensitive, loving, healthy, wealthy or successful . . . we have to learn these habits. So take the next 10 week journey with me to change your attitude about your health and pursue a diet of new thinking and living habits.

STOP START INDEX

CHAPTER ONE Stop negative thinking, start feeling good

CHAPTER TWO Stop eating whatever you desire, start eating for joy

CHAPTER THREE Stop being a couch potato, start being an action hero

CHAPTER FOUR Stop hating your job, sports team, financial situation, start loving your life

CHAPTER FIVE Stop finding fault with others, start finding more friends

CHAPTER SIX Stop being angry with yourself, start feeling good, thinking well and being healthy

CHAPTER SEVEN Stop destructive habits that age you, start learning how to control the subconscious impulses that control us

CHAPTER EIGHT Stop hunting for the better marriage, start renewing your feeling and power of love

CHAPTER NINE Stop hunting for a better job, start working for others' dreams

CHAPTER TEN Stop cynical complaining (about politics, religion, sex, taxes, money and social obstacles to your success), start being a part of the solutions

PLAN YOUR EPITAPH: Never Too Old to Live, Never Too Late to Change by not living this way . . . Never Say Die . . . Always Think Young and the Years will take care of themselves

SELF-HEALTH DEFINED

You are the only one who can determine your life time . . . unless you get run over by a car . . . so the definition of Self-Health is the most important information you can receive:

S cience

E ngineered

L ife

F ulfillment

H ow you think determines your weight

E at when you are hungry and stop when you are full

A ge is not a factor to measure your longevity

L ife is your show and stage so act like it

T ime is a factor in your use of it

H ealth is a journey not a destination

Healthy . . . Body . . . Mind . . . Heart . . . Soul = Self Health

If we follow our conscious minds we will never find true happiness due to acquired habits and attitudes . . . so Self-Health starts with the subconscious mind by stop thinking about failure and start controlling your thoughts through mental exercises that will enable you to accept and enjoy physical exercises . . . these are called affirmations and confirmations stated to yourself in the quiet times . . . when these thoughts become the habit you will find guilt only in the habit of putting them off. "I do not love working out I only feel fulfilled by the act of doing it" . . . Jack Lalanne . . .

the Godfather of Fitness" who lived healthy, happy and prosperous until he was 96.

For a quick reminder just think the 4 w's, who, what, when, where for the first step to self health: who is you, what is your mind, when is now and where is in your own home. Self-Health does not require an exotic gym or setting. Much of my mental exercises are done in bed before I get up in the morning. My weakest moment is when I wake up worrying about the past not planning the future. Many times I have to remind myself that 85% of what I worry about never happens and the other 15% is only half as bad as it seems . . . why should I ruin my day, week and life on 7.5% of my induced worries. My time is much better spent envisioning that "I will" myself to be happy, healthy and prosperous.

Much of religion teaches the very exercises that are proposed in my Self-Health formula. Prayer is envisioning better times and hope . . . hope is the best way to get in an "I Can" mood . . . a good mood is the start of the "I Will" action . . . action is the way to make your future that you envision to stay positive . . . staying positive will put you out front of your life . . . being in front of your life proves that Self-Health works. So, good luck in working on your most valuable asset . . . your mind . . . that will inspire you to work on your body your most neglected asset.

Will this quickly and forever change your outlook, personality, values and ethics . . . no . . . it requires a daily, weekly, monthly, yearly and life long commitment to improving your self worth . . . this is what creates the changes that you yourself want. It takes work.

What if we don't take responsibility for our own health? Then we are doomed by the Boomer Consumers:

- 77.6 million Baby Boomers are generally unhealthy
- Boomers buy 77% of all prescription drugs
- Boomers consume 85% of the health care costs

Self-Health is the only way to quell this socio-economic tsunami.

STOP
START
SIGN

CHAPTER ONE

Mental Exercising

(Stop negative thinking using this book to do
mental exercises, start feeling good)

THOUGHTS ARE THINGS. Your current situation is a result of your thinking, not your circumstances. The experts on behaviors all agree we are what we think we are. But we are what our thinking habits are. If we want to change our thoughts we must CHOOSE to change our thought processes . . . most of which are learned from childhood and have become responses to situations not well thought out consequences.

What is mental exercising? Generally speaking we learn by repetition . . . so by reading and rereading the mental exercises in this book hopefully will start you thinking and acting in a different way. We have been taught, in most instances, what not to do . . . not what to do. That flaws our results. Now we must turn the tables and concentrate on what to do.

There is a story told in baseball about Yogi Berra when he was the skipper for the New York Yankees . . . in the ninth inning of game 7, of the World Series, the opposition had the tying run on base and two outs . . . Yogi goes to the mound to direct the relief pitcher on what to do . . . he proceeded to tell the pitcher "don't throw the ball over the plate" . . . walked back to the dugout and watched the pitcher do the don't thought planted in his head . . . he threw the ball over the plate and the hitter drove it into the seats to win the game.

Yogi was a great catcher but not a successful manager . . . instead of telling the pitcher what to do; "throw the ball outside or inside" he planted a seed of failure in the pitcher's head that created a negative outcome.

A Yogism: In our everyday lives, by replacing the don't words in our subconscious mind (don't eat sugar, fat, starch, calories, carbs, etc.) with the do words (do eat for pleasure, fulfillment, health, fun, love and happiness) we "will seek and find" our more natural being.

What to do is being conscious of our decisions and not letting our subconscious control our lives . . . for it is the subconscious that plays back learned responses based on "what not to do".

You can have a choice if you reprogram responses. So, to change the way we respond to situations not circumstances we must change our subconscious. This will take mental exercising our daily activities in advance in a positive manner.

For example: today is Monday and we have just had a miserable weekend due to anger and disappointment. The mental state is one of dread and dislike for our jobs and current circumstances. The mental state is negative and the day will be negative if approached from this perspective.

When this happens awareness must enter into your mind and take a 180 degree turn for the betterment of your day. So on Monday you will want to forget Saturday and Sunday . . . then knowingly basing the week on better thoughts for better days.

Better thoughts (practice exercises):

- I am happy NOW
- I am healthy NOW
- I am a better person NOW
- I am successful NOW
- I am strong NOW
- I am stress free NOW

Better results (Monday evening):

- I could have been happier today because of

  _____

- I could have been healthier today because of

  _____

- I could have had a better attitude today because of

  _____

- I could have been more successful today because of

  _____

- I could have been stronger today because of

  _____

- I could have been stress free today if I would have

  _____

Better Tomorrow: (repeat the exercises daily or at least weekly and you will be amazed how you improve your stress free aging for results).

However, on Sunday I cannot make up for Monday through Friday indiscretions just through church and prayer. One day of advent cannot make up for 6 days of decent. Lives are gained or lost on religion when it is our life style and heart strings that determine our spirituality. To be good is to be good on Monday through Sunday with our actions and reactions to self control and self affirmations. Our body is our pulpit, our mind is our word, our heart is our haven, our deeds are our tithes, and our spirit is our heaven on earth.

Take the next 10 weeks and change your manner of living using a prescribed "change your life rule" . . . think your way to healthy habits using Self-Health exercises.

Week one   — the thinking diet
Week two   — the living diet
Week three — the working diet
Week four   — the love diet
Week five   — the good will diet
Week six   — the belief diet
Week seven — the stress free diet
Week eight — the happy diet
Week nine   — the giving diet
Week ten   — the wealthy diet

Ten weeks of the Never Too Old diet

STOP
START
SIGN

CHAPTER ONE EXERCISE Stop negative thinking . . . daily affirmations about yourself for your self esteem. Life is positive or negative virtually every day based on your decision to love it or hate it . . . you decide the ride. START: exercise feelings of love and bask in the rewards of happiness.

1) THE WAY YOU THINK IS THE WAY YOU WILL FEEL . . . TO STOP NEGATIVE THINKING IS TO FEEL GOOD ABOUT YOURSELF. THINK IT, FEEL IT.
2) AFFIRM THAT YOU ARE SMART, STRONG, ATTRACTIVE, SUCCESSFUL.
3) FEEL GOOD ABOUT BEING YOUNGER THAN YOUR PEERS.

WEEK ONE—the thinking diet

Monday	walk a mile in your shoes	200 calories burned
Tuesday	ride a bike for a mile any style	300 calories burned
Wednesday	lift your own weight in total resistance , 2 times	300 calories burned
Thursday	do sit-ups/crunches for the size of your waist, 3 times	150 calories burned
Friday	do push ups for the age of your car, 5 times	250 calories burned
Saturday	walk up stairs for the size of your shoes, 4 times	200 calories burned

Sunday	take a respite	each day meditate for the time it takes to go to sleep then recite your best affirmative image. Give thanks for thinking healthy before mentally exercising the right to be happy and quit dreading physical activity. A total of 1,400 calories burned this week.

STOP SMOKING, START LIVING LONGER

Tobacco is no doubt the single most cause of death in the world. *Tobacco kills more then 5 million people which is much much more then HIV/Aids, tuberculosis, malaria combined. By 2030 tobacco is going to kill 8 million people a year. If you smoke you are aging your lungs, heart, liver, digestive system, colon and sex organs at an astounding rate . . . your life expectancy is cut in half as is your nervous system functioning and brain cells.*

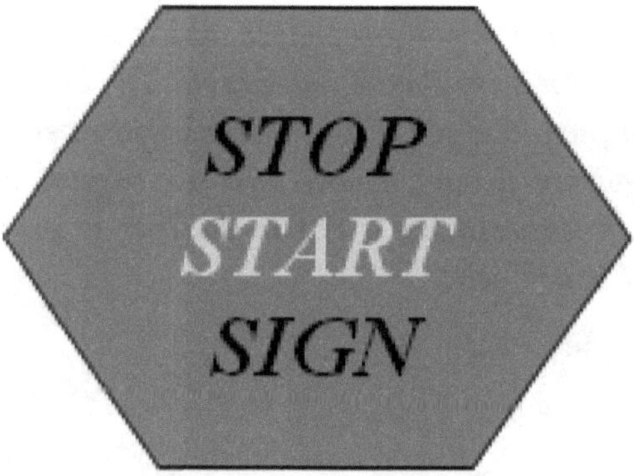
STOP
START
SIGN

Ageless Diet

(Stop eating whatever you desire and use this book
to plan your ageless diet, start eating for joy)

OUR EATING HABITS are also inherited from our past conditioning. Good habits are not the typical pattern of growing up with parents who have bad eating habits. So we have to reprogram our eating habits if we want to; Never be Too Old To LIVE.

I am not one to preach but would like to teach you what I have learned about eating. If it is artificially tasty it is probably not good for you. For instance fast foods, which take the brunt of the bad habits we form, are flavored for instant gratification . . . not permanent health.

Okay this is just common knowledge and sense . . . so how do I break these bad eating habits so I am aging slower and more rewardingly. The fact is I won't live forever, so why shouldn't I just enjoy it and move on? Try being the Biggest User of this book and not the Biggest Loser of this LIFE!

Facts:

- 65% to 70% of Americans are obese or on their way
- 80% of Americans will die before their time
- 90% of Americans do not knowingly strive to live for wellness and fitness
- 100% of Americans eventually die but most due to untimely deaths (always too Young to Die)
- I for one do not want to die before my time, and my time is under my control

I am not going to give you a recipe for what you should eat . . . you know it already . . . we all have it in front of us daily and we just ignore the facts.

But what you can do is this:

- Be conscious of what you are eating
- Look at the labels and plan a better approach to consumption
- At least eat one good meal per day, then two per day, then three . . . a progression is better then no improvement at all
- Keep off the scale and make the reason for healthy eating your age not your weight

A good indicator of your results will be your natural weight, your best energy level, your improved strength, your improved skin and muscle tone, your improved feeling of self worth . . . is it worth it . . . try it. Feeding the body the right nutrients is the quickest route for our spirit to cleanse our soul as well as our pipes.

CAN YOU BELIEVE THIS PERSON WAS 68 IN THIS PICTURE . . . SHE IS NOW 72 AND LOOKS 50 AND ACTS

JERRY RHOADS

AGELESS WITH THAT SMILE … SHE IS PICKY ABOUT WHAT SHE EATS AND EATS WHAT SHE LIKES (WEIGHT 112) … LIKE HER AUNT EDITH AND HER MOTHER DOROTHA, A TRUE MIRACLE AND SHE JUST HAPPENS TO BE MY WIFE OF 52 YEARS.

SHE EATS WHEN SHE IS HUNGRY, EATS ONLY WHAT SHE LIKES AND STOPS EATING WHEN SHE IS FULL … SO DID HER MOTHER WHO DIED PREMATURELY AT 92 AND HER AUNT EDITH WHO LIVED TO BE A RIPE 109.

Death by belt size

Tue, 23 Aug 2011 00:01:00—0500 A study indicates that kidney disease patients with larger waists also have a higher risk of death. Researchers saw it in four years of data on about 5,800 kidney disease patients. At Loyola University Health System in Maywood, Illinois, Holly Kramer compared people with bigger belt sizes with thinner people: ``We noted an approximate twofold increase in mortality risk once waist circumference exceeded 38.5 inches in females or greater than 44 inches in men."

STOP
START
SIGN

CHAPTER TWO EXERCISE Stop eating whatever you desire . . .
START: eating for joy by feeding the soul with daily confirmations
about yourself for your self image.

1) EATING WITHOUT THINKING ABOUT THE
CONSEQUENCES WILL MAKE YOU FEEL HORRIBLE SO
EAT AS IF YOU WERE GOING TO DIE FROM IT.
2) TIME YOUR EATING SO IT DOES NOT CAUSE HASTE
AND WASTE.
3) THINK THIN AND YOU WILL EAT THIN.

WEEK TWO—the living diet

Monday	walk a mile in your shoes	200 calories burned
Tuesday	ride a bike for a mile any style	300 calories burned
Wednesday	lift your own weight in total resistance , 2 times	300 calories burned
Thursday	do sit-ups/crunches for the size of your waist, 3 times	150 calories burned
Friday	do push ups for the age of your car, 5 times	250 calories burned
Saturday	walk up stairs for the size of your shoes, 4 times	200 calories burned

Sunday   take a respite   each day meditate for the time
                                        it takes to go to sleep then
                                        recite your best affirmative
                                        image. Give thanks for
                                        living healthy before
                                        nourishment and eat only
                                        when you are hungry and
                                        quit when you are full. A
                                        total of 1,400 calories
                                        burned this week.

STOP

START

SIGN

CHAPTER THREE

Physical Exercising

(Stop being a couch potato by using this book to do physical exercises, start being an action hero—USE THE DOWNSIZER SPREADSHEET TO PLAN YOUR Body Mass Index—a target for self health) . . . available online at www.nevertoooldtolive.com)

P REACHING WON'T WORK when it comes to getting you to exercise . . . typically Americans do not, will not and can not exercise. Why? Because we do not see the importance of feeling pain . . . because exercise does require some pain. Be it loss of breath, soreness of muscle mass, mental aversion, not enough time, too little results instantly.

I for one have exercised all my life . . . I do not consciously know why . . . I hate the thought of it every day . . . but I do it. Why? I guess it is a habit acquired in my formative years and it has stuck in my subconscious forcing me to feel guilty if I don't do it.

How can you form a feeling of guilt by avoiding the very thing that will allow you to live healthier, longer and in some energy form for ever? Thoughts create action . . . think about getting it over with but feel good after it is. Yes it has to be a habit formed from your desire to live longer. If you do not work on this thought process you will not even live as long as you should. You will die with the following profile:

- At least 50 pounds over your ideal body weight
- At least 4 to 5 chronic diseases
- At least 10 medications per day
- At least some days in a wheel chair
- At least some days in a diaper
- At least 5 years in a nursing home
- At least 10 times per year in the emergency room

- At least 5 times per year admitted to the hospital
- At least 15 times per year to the doctor

This is the fate of at least 65% of Americans and is increasing at an unbelievable rate. Not only does this impact your life it impacts all of our lives . . . the cost of unhealthy Americans is over $3 trillion per year along with the stress of premature dying rather than healthful living.

Just as in mental exercising we must make a personal commitment to change our thinking because that is what changes our daily behavior.

What could the change in behavior be?

1. Walk instead of ride . . . cars, bikes, stairs, jogs, roller skates, roller blades, ice skates
    a. Walking 60 minutes per day burns 300 calories that you would not have burned . . .
    b. that amounts to over 10,000 calories per year or a loss of twenty pounds . . .
    c. in six short months the average American could be at 85% of their best body mass . . .
2. Working in the yard burns 350 calories per hour,
3. Working on or cleaning your own car burns 200 calories per hour
4. Using Wii for exercise games rather than violent games (burns 100's of calories with continued use)
5. Participating in sports (tennis burns 400 calories in an hour, softball burns 300 calories per 7 innings, running burns 400 calories in 30 minutes, bowling burns 200 calories per 10 frames, golf carrying your bag for 18 holes burns 500 calories)
6. Even chewing gum supposedly burns 100 calories an hour . . . that isn't even painful
7. Sleeping well due to keeping well burns stress . . . creates energy
8. Breathing well due to exerting well burns fear . . . creates brain cells
9. Thinking young, believing in self determination burns depression . . . creates hope

What are the odds that you will take this seriously?

- There are 1.7 million patients in nursing homes
- There are 3 million residents in assisted living facilities

- There are 8 billion prescription drugs used annually in nursing homes
- There are 36.1 million admissions annually to hospitals
- There are 123.8 million ER visits to hospitals per year
- There are 77 million fairly unhealthy baby boomers that retire this decade
- There are 550,000 premature deaths in nursing homes every year

What if you do not take this seriously?

- America's health care costs exceed $2 trillion per year
- Life expectancy for the first time ever is going down
- Life expectancy for parents are higher than their children's will be
- More and more of our children will not outlive their parents

Make your choice now or you will never make it . . . if you walk by a crack in the sidewalk once you will never see it again. If you decide to be healthy you will be . . . your mind will take your body there.

The author, in his book Eldercide, points out that aging Americans are being institutionalized against their will when the families can no longer take care of their decline. To remedy Eldercide and Restore Elderpride takes the prevention pill as well as the prescription pill. (I take no pills other than vitamins and plan to avoid institutional care altogether). Annually 550,000 human beings die in nursing homes . . . many, if not most prematurely and costly to the health and welfare of America. It is the responsibility that all of us preserve our health, not destroy it and suffer the consequences . . . . otherwise Eldercide and its devastating losses face us all.

What is the difference between the Medical Model and Health Science anyway? The Medical Model is driven primarily by physicians, hospitals and pharmaceuticals pursing treatment by merely reacting to illness. While Health Science is delving into how the mind heals the body without multi tests, drugs and chemicals by pursing wellness as the desired outcome. Self-Health fits into the scientific methods of prevention and preservation of health over reactionary treatment. Unfortunately, the Health Care Reform movement does not effectively move us towards placebos and natural methods . . . instead private insurers are pursuing Blue Zone Projects that embrace Self-Health science to prevent Red Zone bad habits. The "Blue and Red Zone" movement focuses on how people should live not how they die. And the anti-aging in a pill movement is also suspect since it masks the real reason we age too quickly . . . lack of good natural living habits.

SELF-HEALTH PRACTICED

You are the only one that can determine your life time, weight, happiness and longevity . . . unless you get run over by a car . . . so the practice of Self-Health starts with you:

S cience

E ngineered

L ife

F ulfillment

H ow you think determines your weight

E at when you are hungry and stop when you are full

A ge is not a factor to measure your longevity

L ife is your show and stage so act like it

T ime is a factor in your use of it

H ealth is a journey not a destination

STOP
START
SIGN

CHAPTER THREE EXERCISE Stop being a couch potato . . .
START: daily confirmations about yourself for your self esteem.

1) ONLY YOU CAN CHANGE HABITS FROM BEING INACTIVE TO BEING ACTIVE.
2) SCHEDULE YOUR MENTAL AND PHYSICAL EXERCISE IN FRONT OF YOUR COUCH.
3) WALKING RATHER THAN RIDING, LIFTING RATHER THAN HAULING, STANDING RATHER THAN SITTING . . . LOVING RATHER THAN HATING ALL BURN FAT.

WEEK THREE—the working diet

Monday	walk a mile in your shoes
Tuesday	ride a bike for a mile any style
Wednesday	lift your own weight in total resistance , 2 times
Thursday	do sit-ups/crunches for the size of your waist, 3 times
Friday	do push ups for the age of your car 5 times
Saturday	walk up stairs for the size of your shoes, 4 times
Sunday	take a respite . . . each day meditate for the time it takes to

go to sleep then recite your best affirmative image. Give thanks for being alive and ready to be happy, healthy and prosperous. Make yourself healthy and wealthy . . . they are attached in our minds and hearts. A total of 1,400 calories burned this week. A work out is as much mental as physical . . . enjoy the results not the reason for the work.

CHAPTER FOUR

Positive Actions

(Stop hating your job, sports team, financial situation by using this book
to do creative positive action for happiness, start loving your life)

THE POWER OF positive thinking makes common sense but uncommon among most Americans. We are buried in negativism . . . newspapers, tabloids, television cruelty, movie perversions, gangster rap, violent reality shows, aberrant sexual behaviors, etc, etc.

The world is negative because we tend to see things in a fearful way. We by nature fear the future because of the unknowns. Our own world does not have to be negative but our subconscious has been filled with negativity. To overcome this situation takes acknowledging its existence and a concerted effort to reprogram our subconscious.

How is that possible when we continue to respond when we are confronted by crisis, stress, cynical thoughts, fear, anger, sexual thoughts, false hopes, failures, fantasies, lost dreams, etc, etc.

In my case much of my negative thoughts were about the fear of rejection and being incapable to control my emotions. Success was a pursuit not a result of preparation and dedication. However, they existed from a childhood of little love, support or encouragement . . . my parents were a product of their fears, habits and rejections.

Then came LOVE into my life.

- L ife
- O ccurs
- V irtually in
- E very way

When I found sports I found a way to feel good about my talents . . . I was good at it . . . not excellent but better than most . . . however, I was never the star . . . just the backup or the sixth man. But I had this drive, desire to be the best . . . which spurred me on to this day. I loved it.

This evolved into a reactionary business career. I did very well in school, particularly college but still was not the 4 pointer or the magna cum lade. I was rewarded the highest business award in college. I loved it.

My marriage is very positive and filled the blanks for my lack of love and support from my parents . . . our children are healthy, happy and thrived on my attitude that "can't never did anything" and dreams were to be pursued not squelched. I love it.

My wife and son helped me form a better business after an initial set back. We now are building for the future to assist the elderly to be healthier and have facilities where we are providing restorative services to overcome the bad habits of everyone's earlier years. I love it.

Even though most of my life has resulted in positive results I still feel unfulfilled. Why? Because negativity still lurks in my subconscious . . . I work daily on suppressing the darkness and focusing on the bright lights of tomorrow. Today has already been set in the stone of my past thoughts and actions . . . no changing that . . . but the next day (s) are up to me and my ability to think positively in a negative world. Still I love the challenge.

I get mad at the Cubs and the Bears and America the Beautiful. I rant at the politicians, I wonder about money, I hope for attainment of my goals, I fear the unknown, I am a victim of mood swings . . . I certainly have my negative moments . . . but my study continues on how to keep a positive outlook that results in positive outcomes . . . I read Deepak Chopra, almost daily, I read the Secret at least once a week, I read "The Key To Yourself" as well . . . I work at it. Still I love the Cubs and Bears.

But probably more important I believe I can change my attitude and future if it becomes negative by saying "remember" if you start out negative you will finish the day negative so why would you do it that way . . . and it always works out that the day is dependent on my every morning thinking not just my doing. Just speaking the word love puts you in a positive state of mind.

The next most important function in my daily routines is some form of physical exercise . . . I have been a distance runner (7 miles a day, 7 days per week, 52 weeks per year for 7 years), a rope jumper (counted reps and could jump for an hour without stopping . . . 10,000 reps) a cyclist when I injured my heel from plantar factitious, a weight lifter until I injured my diaphragm, stair stepper, elliptical runner, tread miller, tennis player, etc. All of this was more for keeping my head straight than my physic. I hate the work and love the results.

I never have and never will tell my children or you that you have to exercise to be happy and healthy and prosperous. But I am here to testify that any semblance of success I have had and the fact that I am now 72 years old, have been married 52years to the same great woman (who looks 50 at the age of 71), did 6 sets of 70 pushups for my 4 children and 12 grandchildren and started a new business at the age of 70 are more a product of mental and physical exercise than sheer talent. I love being fit.

Just to let you know I plan to do one set of 80 pushups when I am 80, 90 when I am 90 and 100 when I am 100 . . . after that I plan to slow down. In the next life it is all mental anyway!

Self help books have been an important part of my life . . . early on I was into Earle Nightingale, then Napoleon Hill, now it is The Secret, Depok Chopra; all using some form of human psychology, mentology or scientology. They all carry the same message: you are what you think you are . . . you become what you want to be . . . but random conditioning of your subconscious mind relegates you to your past.

This SELF-HEALTH BOOK forces the issue of moving your thinking in a different path so the future does a mental house cleaning and a new thought conditioning called "I am happy, healthy and prosperous" affirmation enough to replace the subconscious feelings for negativity programmed into all of us by parents, media and life's problems and challenges.

For me mental and physical exercise has enabled me to overcome a negative self image, a fear of the unknown, because I now can control my thoughts about what I want and it will appear as it has for many others.

You become what you feel good about . . . feelings dictate success and health. If you think about it every invention, accomplishment, miracle starts with an idea . . . your creative thinking drives your health and wealth. Abundance is created by your thoughts not lotto or luck.

**STOP
START
SIGN**

CHAPTER FOUR EXERCISE Stop hating your job, sports team, financial situation . . . START: daily confirmations about yourself for your self FULFILLMENT. HATE IS NEGATIVE THINKING THAT MAKES YOU UNHAPPY . . . BEING HAPPY STOPS THE HATING . . . TRY IT YOU WILL LOVE IT.

1) LOVE IS THE CURE EVEN THOUGH YOU DON'T KNOW IT . . . JUST CHANGING YOUR PERCEPTION CURES THE HATE. LOVE YOUR FELLOW MAN AND PEACE WILL COME TO THE WORLD.
2) LOVE YOUR JOB HATE UNEMPLOYMENT, LOVE YOUR TEAM HATE CHOOSING ANOTHER TEAM, LOVE YOUR LIFE AND MONEY WILL FOLLOW.
3) MONEY AND WEALTH FLOW TO THOSE WHO BELIEVE THEY DESERVE TO BE WEALTHY.

WEEK FOUR—the love diet

Monday	walk a mile in your shoes
Tuesday	ride a bike for a mile any style
Wednesday	lift your own weight in total resistance, 2 times
Thursday	do sit-ups/crunches for the size of your waist, 3 times
Friday	do push ups for the age of your car 5 times
Saturday	walk up stairs for the size of your shoes, 4 times
Sunday	take a respite . . . each day meditate for the time it takes to

go to sleep then recite your best affirmative image. Give thanks for being a self fulfilling prophesy of a whole, healthy, happy and prosperous person. A total of 1,400 calories burned this week. Making love burns more calories than hating life.

CHAPTER FIVE

Finding Good

(Stop finding fault with others by using this book to find good in everyone, start finding more friends)

GOOD WILL HUNTING was a successful film, story and won Oscars for Matt Damon and Ben Affleck and turned their lives around. The messages that the film portrayed are meaningful to all of us . . . we all have a God Given Talent that needs expression . . . if you do not express it you will suffer the frustration of being unfulfilled.

From that film the word "Karma" comes to mind which is your good will planting of the seeds of self worth and "Dharma" which is your good will finding and harvesting the good in your life. We then can be truly happy, healthy and prosperous in our daily LIFE.

America is addicted to athletes and celebrities to the extent that they become folk heroes without usually earning the role. We find out later that they are just ordinary people doing extra ordinary things because they believe they can. That is the reason I kept reminding my children to pursue their dreams and that "can't never did anything" and "can discovered America and Americans discovered GOOD WILL HUNTING.

Will Hunting was wasting his talent on being one of the boys in the hood but was a genius mathematician who would never have been discovered if Robin Williams had not taken him by the head and straightened him into a wonderful success story. Who will be your mentor . . . have you found one yet. They are out there waiting for you to want to be good enough to think and grow rich. This is called the Law of Attraction . . . likes attract likes.

Well you have to be looking or have opportunity take you there because most of us do not have the awareness to recognize our special talents let alone capitalize on them. In my case I went from being a bored auditor to becoming a health care expert because the company I worked for said I could, and would not accept anything less. But my first mentor was a Rabbi who owned nursing homes and he spotted my talent . . . knowledge about the Medicare programs and enlisted my expertise in his businesses . . . he let me practice on his playground and he paid me for it.

After taking on his facilities and turning them around I worked myself out of a job at the age of 45, and met my next mentor who had responsibilities for 50 long term care facilities and I was hired as a consultant to turn-a-round the worst of the worst. I again worked myself out of a job and at the age of 47 went back into my own business.

I found these two gentlemen who believed in me and my talent . . . it then inspired me to take on a new business at the age of 70 to practice what I have learned so I can help the elderly and disabled have a quality of life . . . extend their lives not just end them.

My wife and son are my partners and we are committed to finding a good way to manage the aging process for ourselves and our patients. And through the Law of Attraction (likes attract likes) we plan to build a franchise business that will serve aging Americans in a positive and stimulating environment.

> Looking back I feel I was destined to find good expression of my talents because my first memories of the elderly was a rest home across from my house in Indianola, Iowa . . . these poor souls were spending all day in rocking chairs with nothing to do or live for . . . to me that seemed wrong and it still does. And now I can do something about it.

The D. C. Whitehouse (named after Shari's mother Dorotha Corny White) is our dream house dedicated to changing the lives of aging America through better life actions by planning and pre-forming attitudes about age. We need to become a nation of health preservers not life preservers . . . this all starts in our home with our children and their habits . . . ironically their habits are your habits . . . like it or not the future of our children is set in motion by our feelings and actions about ourselves and others. The ripple effect of you becoming happy, healthy and prosperous is amazing for the future of your children and America in general.

Another positive result of our finding good in others will affect our spouse who is the very foundation of our sexuality and family. For eternal happiness and health we must find the chemistry with someone to make our sexuality come on and live on. That is not the pure sex that pornography leads us into . . . it is the connection that love requires for creating offspring and an on spring to feeling good about ourselves. Shari and I are promoting Self-Health as a means to that end . . . health, happiness and sexuality as a part of life's prosperity. To do that you need, a body that is physically attractive, a mind that is morally straight and a life style that is positive and fulfilled. We believe that is the right of being human whether we are hetro, gay or any other sexual label.

STOP
START
SIGN

CHAPTER FIVE EXERCISE Stop finding fault with others . . .
START: daily confirmations about yourself for your self esteem.

1) LOVE THY NEIGHBOR AND FIND FRIENDS TO LIKE AND JOY WILL REPLACE STRESS.
2) WIDEN YOUR CIRCLE AND EMBRACE GIVING AND RECEIVING GOOD WILL AND IT WILL FIND YOU.
3) BRING A GIFT AND BLESSING TO ALL YOU MEET AND GREET.

WEEK FIVE—the good will diet

Monday	walk a mile in your shoes, then kiss your spouse
Tuesday	ride any style bike a mile, then complement your spouse
Wednesday	lift your own weight in total, then lift up your spouse, 2 times
Thursday	do sit-ups/crunches for the size of your waist, 3 times
Friday	do push ups for the age of your car 5 times
Saturday	walk up stairs for the size of your shoes, 4 times
Sunday	take a respite . . . each day meditate for the time it takes to

go to sleep then recite your best affirmative image. A total of 1,400 calories burned this week.

And for your own good will finding respect your mate as yourself each day by noticing his or her beauty, good traits, given talents, contribution to your life, by giving thanks for all of these things that we may have taken for granted. Amen

CHAPTER SIX

Self Worth Capital

(Stop being angry with yourself by using this book to see your self worth, start feeling good, thinking well and being healthy)

OVER THE AGES man has asked man what am I worth . . . never realizing that worth is determined by one's self not those around us. When we are worthy we attract more worth until we are wealthy.

Why do we ask others when the answer is usually couched in what the other person thinks of themselves . . . if they are unhappy with themselves we will not and can not get any positive feedback from them . . . if they are happy with themselves they don't want to make it any easier for you then they had it . . . so guess what . . . the truth is in the ears of the listener not in the voice of the speaker. You make your own self worth minute by minute, hour by hour, day by day.

The saying is "mental attitude has more to do with success than mental capacity" . . . if you want it bad enough it shall be yours. But most people do look outside themselves for encouragement, fulfillment, love, understanding, support, faith, endearment, etc. etc. Do they find it there? That is the question that we need to answer.

Who is your best friend? Does he or she really know all your thoughts about them and yourself? If they did they would not be your friend. We do not live out our thoughts . . . we hide behind them and rationalize them so we do not offend others nor expose ourselves. Most of those thoughts are negative due to a lack of recognition and cognition that we are what we think we are.

To build our self net worth we need to invest our self worth capital in developing knowledge, faith, love, loyalty, honesty, commitment, expectations on what is right for others as well as ourselves. The beggar is repulsive and rejected because we see ourselves in them and fear those consequences of bad luck and avoid feeling good about our own good luck. By giving to the beggar we can feel good about our good luck regardless of how the money is used.

True Giving opens the heart not the pocketbook . . . if it is about affording a gift it is not a gift it is a sacrifice and that does not build self worth it erodes self respect.

Can we give enough to feel good about ourselves? Most times the act is for a reason other than being good to others. Americans during this depressed economy are withdrawing into themselves to protect their pride and livelihood. This is the time we can reap the most from our giving because there are always those who are worse off . . . the very act will make our value increase in our heart and leave the payment of bills to our head. We then will have more coming than going by doing good.

This is not just a religious concept it is the Law of Attraction at work again . . . good attracts good . . . need generates a use of our talents . . . demand for our talents increases our net self worth. That is what generates dollars and makes human value into capital for our children and grandchildren.

The free enterprise concept of the Law of Attraction is bankruptcy which is America's willingness to allow us to fail then rekindle our fire and do what our dreams want us to do . . . yes it is 100% mental . . . everything starts with an idea, a thought and a vision . . . you can be either the envision(er) or the envision(ee) but the point is you decide. Either way you are allowed to fail then reorganize and succeed . . . no other economic system allows for this. This is the greatest part of capitalism versus the other isms . . . we are allowed to freely choose to fail then choose to succeed . . . just remember it is all founded on how you think and what you want to be.

However, we have been brain washed that capitalism is free enterprise allowing us to pursue opportunities without fear of failure . . . that is misleading from my experience . . . I have had sleepless nights since I started my own business in April 1977 because I had no other choice . . . I was fired from my job and left in the darkness of my future. Then and there my mind's self capital started its own business. What capitalism means to me is a way to capitalize on my dreams, talents and work ethic. It is not a freedom based on money, cash flow and profits. It is freedom to try, make creative thought come alive and invest in timing the market. Then money and cash flows from profit. We then are happy to pay taxes, make contributions as a benefactor and support capitalism.

So Self-Health drives enterprise in all facets of our life . . . family, success, ideals, hope and the leverage that money brings to the future. In some political circles, the misinterpretation, in my opinion, is that Capitalism is an exercise in selfishness . . . my interpretation is that Capitalism at its worst is far better than the other ism's and gives us the right to retain our individuality (freedom).

STOP
START
SIGN

CHAPTER SIX EXERCISE Stop being angry with yourself . . .
START: daily confirmations about yourself for your self capital.

1) YOU ARE THE ONE AND ONLY YOU . . .NO ONE ON EARTH IS EXACTLY LIKE YOU . . . LOOK AROUND, YOU ARE TOTALLY UNIQUE AND TALENTED IN A UNIQUE WAY . . . CAPITALIZE ON THAT.
2) ANGER IN THE MORNING DESTROYS ANY CHANCE OF HAVING A GOOD DAY . . . START OUT RIGHT AND THINGS GO RIGHT.
3) BELIEVE IN YOUR SELF BY BELIEVING YOUR THOUGHTS CREATE ALL THAT YOU HAVE EVER WANTED.

WEEK SIX—the belief diet

Monday	walk a mile in your shoes
Tuesday	ride a bike for a mile any style
Wednesday	lift your own weight in total resistance, 2 times
Thursday	do sit-ups/crunches for the size of your waist, 3 times
Friday	do push ups for the age of your car 5 times
Saturday	walk up stairs for the size of your shoes, 4 times
Sunday	take a respite . . . each day meditate for the time it takes to

go to sleep then recite your best affirmative image. "Give thanks for your good life" and think of ways to give joy to others. A total of 1,400 calories burned this week believing in your self-health plan.

STOP
START
SIGN

CHAPTER SEVEN

Master Of Good Habits

(Stop destructive habits that age you by using this book to form good habits, learn how to control the subconscious impulses day by day listening to your own affirmations . . . start ideas and thoughts then create your world)

CAPTAIN OF MY self made state, Master of My fate. Am I really in control of my destiny? Or is it some supreme being that has me on a puppet string? It is whatever you decide . . . you are master of your thoughts if you decide to be and then you are captain of your fate. Destiny is never fixed and circumstances are determined by the past . . . so invest today wisely since it will determine where you are tomorrow. Your mental capacity is unlimited (President JFK had an ordinary IQ and an extraordinary EQ . . . so do you).

We started out speaking of good habits and have spent most chapters on that topic . . . the topic of you. YOU are the center of your world, your universe, your future . . . that is the exciting knowledge that I have learned through hours upon hours of reading and thinking and meditating. Though fear drove me most of the time:

- Fear of failure
- Fear of not being able to pay my bills
- Fear of not being accepted (rejection)
- Fear of dying early
- Fear of living less
- Fear of the fear itself

I succeeded in squelching the fear through mental and physical exercises. I am not saying "if I can do it you can" that is condescending at the very least . . . I am encouraging you to over come fear by changing how you think about yourself. This takes changing your routines, your habits, your actions, your future by changing your NOW . . . the past is gone and needs to be buried because that is not you NOW.

Pick a book . . . it is not a come down to find the answers in knowledge or GOOD WILL HUNTING adventures. It is reeducating your subconscious to be what you want to be . . . want is the main ingredient . . . not money . . . not talent . . . not relationships . . . not love . . . those are results of you exercising your right to want, give and receive your desires, your dreams, your goals.

Being a master at anything takes, according to Malcolm Gladwell, a minimum of 10,000 hours (5 continuous years) of training and preparation . . . athletes, scientists, performers, politicians, attorneys, business entrepreneurs, physicians, if they are any good at all, have to study and go into a timeless obsession to be the best at something and then they are what they are. You are what you expect to be and want to be . . . master your good habits, be not your bad habits, by being stress free from doubt:

- Decide that you can overcome your fears . . . state them then confront them, climb the mountain of doubt
- Set simple goals that can be accomplished then savor more ambitious successes, in your daily life
- Find a place for your self satisfaction in giving to others and loving your present life, with presents and gifts for those in need
- Prepare each day with a healthy agenda (age-nda means a health plan for the day including food, exercise, thoughts of love, acts of kindness) giving away not just taking away
- Stick your neck out for causes you stand for then take action to help others find their age-nda, using this book

No matter how many books are written on Self-Help or Self-Engineering none can be complete without putting the most important ingredient first . . . that is the commitment to family . . . to marriage regardless of sexual orientation . . . to offspring and to wellspring. Yes commitment; not let's try and see if it works . . . it will work if you work for it . . . divorce is the most destructive force we have in America for negativity, loss of health, loss of wealth, loss of dignity and loss of our children's future.

Yes commitment to one's responsibility to self and others is the science of Self-Health.

No I am not foolish enough to say every marriage is going to work . . . that is not realistic . . . however, that is not a bad idea for most who want happiness, health and prosperity. Otherwise the reverse typically results . . . unhappiness, unhealthiness and financial setbacks. However, a change of mates that leads to happiness in pursuit of self-health is worthy and necessary.

STOP START SIGN

CHAPTER SEVEN EXERCISE Stop destructive habits that age you . . . START: daily confirmations about yourself for your self esteem.

1) DESTROY STRESS IN YOUR LIFE AND GOOD HABITS WILL FOLLOW YOU WHEREVER YOU GO. THINKING WELL OF YOURSELF WILL DESTROY STRESS AND STIMULATE LOVE.
2) LIVE UP TO YOUR DREAMS, LIVE DOWN YOUR FEARS SO YOUR NEVER ACCEPTING THAT IT IS BAD LUCK . . . GOOD LUCK IS PREPARATION AND BELIEF MEETING OPPORTUNITY.
3) THINKING AND WANTING ARE POSITIVE STEPS TO GETTING AND RECEIVING . . . SO THINK BIG, WANT BIG AND THE WILL TO BE BIG IS TURNED ON.

WEEK SEVEN—the stress free diet

Monday	walk a mile in your shoes
Tuesday	ride a bike for a mile any style
Wednesday	lift your own weight in total resistance, 2 times
Thursday	do sit-ups/crunches for the size of your waist, 3 times
Friday	do push ups for the age of your car 5 times
Saturday	walk up stairs for the size of your shoes, 4 times
Sunday	take a respite . . . each day meditate for the time it takes

to go to sleep then recite your best affirmative image. Reduce stress by conceiving and achieving your self-health goals. A total of 1,400 calories burned this week.

CHAPTER EIGHT

Hunting Relationships

(Stop hunting for the better marriage by using this book to find the best in your current relationships, start renewing your feeling and power of love)

ARE YOU EVER happy with your situation or your job? If not how can you be happy with your wife, children, friends and self. Happiness should not come last . . . it has to come first for you to have good health and prosperity. You can be rich in dollars and poor in health and relationships.

Is this speculation or fact? Look again at the statistics:

- Divorces, over 50% of those who marry get divorced
- Drug use, over 75% of those depressed actively use drugs, alcohol or substances to drop out
- Life expectancy
  - ° Females 80
  - ° Males 70
- Retirement
  - ° Females 62
  - ° Males 65
- Unemployment 9.3%
- Underemployment 16%
- Obesity 63%

Signs and symptoms of your emerging true youth:

- Happy
- Healthy
- Prosperous
- Faithful

- Positive
- Goal Seeking

What's your emotional and mental age now after 7 weeks of Self-Health study and exercises?

If you are still emotionally old remember to recast your thinking so the sun is not setting on your future because no hope, no job, no marriage, no relationships, no life . . . If you are mentally old, the moon has eclipsed on your past, no dreams fulfilled, no love gained, no successful events, no joyful memories, no happy bed time stories, no value of life as you know it.

This state of affairs can and must be reversed for you to age naturally and happy and healthy, and prosperous. Many will just accept unhappiness as happenstance that one must endure, while in waiting for happenstance to change. Guess what, it does not happen if your stance is on blaming others or just good ole circumstance. Good luck on making that work.

The cure is, as always, in your head . . . you either think young or feel old . . . why not feel young and forget thinkin' old.

America is on the threshold of disaster economically, politically and emotionally due to the disintegration of the family unit. The dissolving of the most important of all relationships . . . marriage . . . be it same sex or not . . . we must reverse this trend or continue to be the rise and fall of America as was the Roman Empire, the Mayan Empire, the British Empire, etc.

Each individual in America must rethink their values using knowledge, study, thoughtful meditation and leadership . . . we can no longer leave this up to Government to dictate and police. Individual freedoms come from individual effort and we must go back to some basic values to repair what intellectual dominance has caused:

- Free to choose jobs
- Free to choose careers
- Free to choose leaders that value character
- Free to choose religious thought
- Free to take up arms only in our defense
- Free to represent peace rather than war

- Free to have housing, education and a standard of living that is experienced in varying degrees to all
- Free to pay taxes for the benefit of all
- Free to elect officials that are reachable and accountable to the voters.

Whether it be Democrat or Republican we need a more contrasting school of thought that takes us back to the founding fathers position that Government can be a blessing or a burden unless it is being reconstituted with new thought and representatives every 4 to 8 years . . . we have completely lost this with the advent of career politicians, state officials and their offspring dominating the power and funding to their benefit not the benefit of those that pay the majority of the bills, including their personal nest egg.

Einstein is famous for the theory of relativity as it applies to Science and it applies here: everything in humanity is relative to the acts of the majority and the minority shall not reject that for their own benefit.

Think again about this before you think about yourself:

- 10% of the people lead the 90%
- 90% of the people would like to lead but don't
- Why not?
  - Fear of the unknown
  - Not goal driven
  - Not prepared
  - Not risk takers
- What does this have to do with aging?
  - Fear causes stress that causes premature aging
  - Goals are set but not pursued causing disappointment, stress and aging
  - Little or no preparation causes failure, stress and aging
  - Allowing ego to prevail causes selfishness, stress and aging
  - Hiding behind excuses due to risk of rejection causes, hesitancy, stress and aging

Eliminate the above negatives and live for a stress free ageless life. Get involved and make a difference in your life, in America and the world.

Shari and I met in Indianola High School. She says she spotted me and I know that is not true because I spotted her when I was an eight grader and she was in seventh. The significance of who spotted who first is lost in the next 55+ years that we have been together.

Yes it is unique these days for baseball pitchers to win 20 games and marriages to last 50, 60, 70, 80 years . . . the world record seems to be 91 so we all have a ways to go.

My parents were married 55 years, but due to poor health they expired in their 80's in nursing homes that were despicable to say the least. Shari's father died of cancer at the age of 66 much like Shari's sister.

On the other hand the oldest person on record was 122 and the top 100 are the product of being happy, healthy and wealthy in their life styles regardless of race, creed or religion:

Rank	Name	Sex	Birth date	Death date	Age	Country of death
1	Jeanne Calment	F	21 February 1875	4 August 1997	122 years, 164 days	France
2	Shigechiyo Izumi	M	29 June 1865	21 February 1986	120 years, 237 days[1]	Japan
3	Sarah Knauss	F	24 September 1880	30 December 1999	119 years, 97 days	United States
4	Lucy Hannah	F	16 July 1875	21 March 1993	117 years, 248 days	United States
5	Marie-Louise Meilleur	F	29 August 1880	16 April 1998	117 years, 230 days	Canada
6	María Capovilla	F	14 September 1889	27 August 2006	116 years, 347 days	Ecuador
7	Tane Ikai	F	18 January 1879	12 July 1995	116 years, 175 days	Japan
8	Elizabeth Bolden	F	15 August 1890	11 December 2006	116 years, 118 days	United States
9	Carrie C. White	F	18 November 1874	14 February 1991	116 years, 88 days[2]	United States
10	Kamato Hongo	F	16 September 1887	31 October 2003	116 years, 45 days[3]	Japan
11	Maggie Barnes	F	6 March 1882	19 January 1998	115 years, 319 days	United States

12	Christian Mortensen	M	16 August 1882	25 April 1998	115 years, 252 days	United States[a]
13	Charlotte Hughes	F	1 August 1877	17 March 1993	115 years, 228 days	United Kingdom
14	Edna Parker	F	20 April 1893	26 November 2008	115 years, 220 days	United States
15	Margaret Skeete	F	27 October 1878	7 May 1994	115 years, 192 days	United States
16	Gertrude Baines	F	6 April 1894	11 September 2009	115 years, 158 days	United States
17	Ani ica Butariu	F	17 June 1882	21 November 1997	115 years, 157 days[4]	Romania
18	Emiliano Mercado del Toro	M	21 August 1891	24 January 2007	115 years, 156 days	Puerto Rico
19	Bettie Wilson	F	13 September 1890	13 February 2006	115 years, 153 days	United States
20	Julie Winnefred Bertrand	F	16 September 1891	18 January 2007	115 years, 124 days	Canada
21	Maria de Jesus	F	10 September 1893	2 January 2009	115 years, 114 days	Portugal
22	Susie Gibson	F	31 October 1890	16 February 2006	115 years, 108 days	United States
23	Hendrikje van Andel-Schipper	F	29 June 1890	30 August 2005	115 years, 62 days	Netherlands
24	Maude Farris-Luse	F	21 January 1887	18 March 2002	115 years, 56 days	United States
25	Marie Brémont	F	25 April 1886	6 June 2001	115 years, 42 days	France
26	Annie Jennings	F	12 November 1884	20 November 1999	115 years, 8 days	United Kingdom
27	Eva Morris	F	8 November 1885	2 November 2000	114 years, 360 days	United Kingdom
28	Kama Chinen	F	10 May 1895	2 May 2010	114 years, 357 days	Japan
29	Mary Bidwell	F	19 May 1881	25 April 1996	114 years, 342 days	United States
30	Mary Josephine Ray	F	17 May 1895	7 March 2010	114 years, 294 days	United States[b]
31	Maria do Couto Maia-Lopes	F	24 October 1890	25 July 2005	114 years, 274 days	Portugal
32	Ramona Trinidad Iglesias-Jordan	F	31 August 1889	29 May 2004	114 years, 272 days	Puerto Rico

33	Eugénie Blanchard	F	16 February 1896	Living	114 years, 249 days	France
34	Neva Morris	F	3 August 1895	6 April 2010	114 years, 246 days	United States
35	Hide Ohira	F	15 September 1880	9 May 1995	114 years, 236 days	Japan
36	Mathew Beard	M	9 July 1870	16 February 1985	114 years, 222 days[5]	United States
37	Yone Minagawa	F	4 January 1893	13 August 2007	114 years, 221 days	Japan
38	M.A.C.C.[6]	F	10 June 1881	16 January 1996	114 years, 220 days	Spain
39	Carrie Lazenby	F	9 February 1882	14 September 1996	114 years, 218 days	United States
	Ura Koyama	F	30 August 1890	5 April 2005	114 years, 218 days	Japan
41	Myrtle Dorsey	F	22 November 1885	25 June 2000	114 years, 216 days	United States
42	Anna Eliza Williams	F	2 June 1873	27 December 1987	114 years, 208 days	United Kingdom
43	Grace Clawson	F	15 November 1887	28 May 2002	114 years, 194 days	United States[c]
44	Tase Matsunaga	F	11 May 1884	18 November 1998	114 years, 191 days	Japan
45	Yukichi Chuganji	M	23 March 1889	28 September 2003	114 years, 189 days	Japan
46	Lydie Vellard	F	18 March 1875	17 September 1989	114 years, 183 days	France
	Wilhelmina Kott	F	7 March 1880	6 September 1994	114 years, 183 days	United States
	Adelina Domingues	F	19 February 1888	21 August 2002	114 years, 183 days	United States[d]
49	Mitoyo Kawate	F	15 May 1889	13 November 2003	114 years, 182 days	Japan
50	Charlotte Benkner	F	16 November 1889	14 May 2004	114 years, 180 days	United States[e]
	Camille Loiseau	F	13 February 1892	12 August 2006	114 years, 180 days	France
52	Anne Primout	F	5 October 1890	26 March 2005	114 years, 172 days	France[f]
53	Ettie Mae Greene	F	8 September 1877	26 February 1992	114 years, 171 days	United States

54	Irene Frank	F	1 October 1881	28 February 1996	114 years, 150 days	United States
55	Christina Cock	F	25 December 1887	22 May 2002	114 years, 148 days	Australia
56	Olivia Patricia Thomas	F	29 June 1895	16 November 2009	114 years, 140 days	United States
57	Emma Verona Johnston	F	6 August 1890	1 December 2004	114 years, 117 days	United States
58	Bettie Chatmon	F	30 April 1884	16 August 1998	114 years, 108 days	United States
59	Odie Matthews	F	28 December 1878	14 April 1993	114 years, 107 days	United States
60	Chiyo Shiraishi	F	6 August 1895	19 November 2009	114 years, 105 days	Japan
61	Eunice Sanborn	F	20 July 1896	Living	114 years, 95 days	Living in the United States
62	Asa Takii	F	28 April 1884	31 July 1998	114 years, 94 days	Japan
63	Florence Knapp	F	10 October 1873	11 January 1988	114 years, 93 days	United States
	Elena Slough	F	4 July 1889	5 October 2003	114 years, 93 days	United States
65	Lucy Jane Askew	F	8 September 1883	9 December 1997	114 years, 92 days	United Kingdom
	Mary Anna Boone	F	10 February 1887	13 May 2001	114 years, 92 days	United States
67	M.C.L.L.[6]	F	3 April 1883	3 July 1997	114 years, 91 days	Spain
68	Waka Shirahama	F	23 March 1878	16 June 1992	114 years, 85 days	Japan
69	Joan Riudavets	M	15 December 1889	5 March 2004	114 years, 81 days	Spain
70	Suekiku Miyanaga	F	7 April 1884	20 June 1998	114 years, 74 days	Japan
71	Maggie Renfro	F	14 November 1895	22 January 2010	114 years, 69 days	United States
72	Emma Tillman	F	22 November 1892	28 January 2007	114 years, 67 days	United States
73	Besse Cooper	F	26 August 1896	Living	114 years, 58 days	Living in the United States
74	Florrie Baldwin	F	31 March 1896	8 May 2010	114 years, 38 days	United Kingdom

75	Walter Breuning	M	21 September 1896	Living	114 years, 32 days	Living in the United States
76	Amy Isabel Hulmes	F	5 October 1887	27 October 2001	114 years, 22 days	United Kingdom
77	Grace Thaxton	F	18 June 1891	6 July 2005	114 years, 18 days	United States
78	Minnie Ward	F	19 November 1885	2 December 1999	114 years, 13 days	United States
79	Arbella Ewing	F	13 March 1894	22 March 2008	114 years, 9 days	United States
80	Catherine Hagel	F	28 November 1894	6 December 2008	114 years, 8 days	United States
81	Virginia Dighero	F	24 December 1891	28 December 2005	114 years, 4 days	Italy
82	Fred Hale	M	1 December 1890	19 November 2004	113 years, 354 days	United States
83	Miriam Carpelan	F	8 July 1882	22 June 1996	113 years, 350 days	United States[g]
84	Yasu Akino	F	1 March 1885	12 February 1999	113 years, 348 days	Japan
	Bertha Fry	F	1 December 1893	14 November 2007	113 years, 348 days	United States
86	Mae Harrington	F	20 January 1889	29 December 2002	113 years, 343 days	United States
87	Daisey Bailey	F	30 March 1896	7 March 2010	113 years, 342 days	United States
88	Chiyono Hasegawa	F	20 November 1896	Living	113 years, 337 days	Living in Japan
89	Agatha Mitchell	F	26 March 1887	25 February 2001	113 years, 336 days	United States
90	Moses Hardy	M	6 January 1893	7 December 2006	113 years, 335 days[z]	United States
91	Venere Pizzinato	F	23 November 1896	Living	113 years, 334 days	Living in Italy[h]
92	Clara Huhn	F	28 January 1887	20 December 2000	113 years, 327 days	United States
93	Corinne Dixon Taylor	F	2 April 1893	14 February 2007	113 years, 318 days	United States
94	Mary Christian	F	12 June 1889	20 April 2003	113 years, 312 days	United States

95	Luce Maced	F	2 May 1886	25 February 2000	113 years, 299 days	France
96	Rosa Ann Comfort	F	21 January 1879	6 November 1992	113 years, 290 days	United Kingdom
97	Fannie Thomas	F	14 April 1867	22 January 1981	113 years, 283 days	United States
	Mitsu Fujisawa	F	9 April 1876	17 January 1990	113 years, 283 days[8]	Japan
99	Shige Hirooka	F	16 January 1897	Living	113 years, 280 days	Living in Japan
100	Tsuneyo Toyonaga	F	21 May 1894	22 February 2008	113 years, 277 days	Japan

Source: Google

The United States is tops with 50 centenarians, Japan a distant second with 17, then United Kingdom with 8, France with 7, Puerto Rico with 2, China with none reported (but rumored to have millions), Russia with none reported; 7 of these centurions are still living. . . . how would you like to crack the top 100 oldest . . . I would.

Right now only 5 are males and 95 are females but life styles will dictate longevity so females will likely die younger and life expectancy for females will plateau.

STOP
START
SIGN

CHAPTER EIGHT EXERCISE Stop hunting for the better marriage . . . START: daily confirmations about yourself for your ageless self-health.

1. LOOK AT WHAT YOU HAVE BEFORE YOU LOOK AT WHAT YOU DON'T HAVE AND YOU MAY DISCOVER HAPPINESS IS BETTER THAN STRESS.
2. LOVE CONQUERS FEAR AND FEAR IS THE ROOT OF DIVORCE . . . WE FEAR LOSING OUR LOVE TO SOMEONE ELSE AND DON'T BRING IT TO OUR SPOUSE EVERY DAY . . . JUST DO IT!
3. FINDING THE PERFECT MATCH ISN'T EVEN CLOSE TO BEING POSSIBLE . . . FINDING THE PERFECT CHEMISTRY LIES IN YOUR ATTITUDE TOWARDS GIVE AND TAKE . . . GIVE AND YOU WILL RECEIVE . . . TAKE AND YOU WILL LOSE.

WEEK EIGHT—the happy diet

Monday   walk a mile in your shoes
Tuesday   ride a bike for a mile any style
Wednesday   lift your own weight in total resistance, 2 times
Thursday   do sit-ups/crunches for the size of your waist, 3 times
Friday   do push ups for the age of your car 5 times
Saturday   walk up stairs for the size of your shoes, 4 times
Sunday   take a respite . . . each day meditate for the time it takes to go to sleep then recite your best affirmative image. Be happy that your self-health is connected to the Universal mind and you are eternally an energy field in this master plan. A total of 1,400 calories burned this week.

STOP
START
SIGN

CHAPTER NINE

Exercise Giving

(Stop hunting for a better job by using this book to exercise giving to your current job, start by using this book to work for others' dreams)

M Y WIFE IS the most giving person I have known . . . as a result everyone around her respects her opinion and her actions because she is "we centered not me centered."

I have to work every day at being as good as she is . . . her first thought is of the other person. My first thought tends to be about my wishes, dreams and goals. Together we have built a wonderful life of having it out every six months because I step out of the acceptable bounds of what is reasonable and likely to happen . . . the dreamer brought down to earth. She the, GOOD WILL FINDER, stating the obvious being considerate for all involved, not just my limited perception and far out vision.

To be a good giver you must exercise the will to be good not just an "emotion giver". The emotion giver gives for personal reasons such as a disaster needing contributions, a tip for a table, a shallow commitment for volunteerism, small gifts to the pan handler, etc.

The traits of my wife the GOOD GIVER:

- Doesn't consider the amount as being a factor
- Responds to need not who is needy
- Follows through on volunteer work
- Doesn't say no to the kids, grandkids or in laws
- Brings a present whenever she feels like giving, which is on all occasions, including vacation shopping for trinkets
- Always says yes to requests for the check

As a result she is ageless, she is beauty, she is the smile that lights up the room, she is the center of our family's root system and my wings. God has blessed us with her, her mother and her mother's mother who were all givers. I am still learning the act of giving . . . not just advice as I am attempting to do in this book . . . but actually being better at being a human being:

1. Look past self for my net worth
2. Take time to volunteer
3. Take time to get involved in Governing
4. Take time to make a difference in the life of aging America
5. Be active in bringing America back to a giving country standing for peace rather than a threatening force using imperialism . . . which means less military and more charity to those that need liberty but don't want it

- **G** ifts

- **I** mprove

- **V** irtually

- **E** verything

Sam Walton in his book "Made in America" stated that his only regret was not discovering the power of sharing his wealth with his employees (associates) earlier. America's wealthy give more away than they keep. However, they do not usually re-invest in re-capitalizing the very economy they profited from . . . i.e., paying taxes on net worth, not net adjusted gross income. Taxes should, at the same time be used to re-capitalize America's entrepreneurs not wasted on bigger government and oppressive regulations.

STOP START SIGN

CHAPTER NINE EXERCISE Stop hunting for a better job . . .
START: daily confirmations about yourself for the greater good of society.

1. BETTER, BEST AND BEYOND BELIEF IS JUST THAT . . .
   JOBS ARE NOT FOR CHOOSING UNTIL YOU HAVE
   MASTERED YOUR JOB OF GOOD FINDING . . . LOOK
   FOR GOOD IN EVERYTHING AND YOU WILL FIND IT.
   GIVE AND YOU WILL RECEIVE.
2. CHILDREN ARE NEVER LOOKING FOR BETTER THEY
   ARE LOOKING FOR FUN AND THEY ARE LOOKING FOR A
   GOOD TIME . . . AS WE GROW OLD FROM STRESS WE HAVE
   FORGOTTEN THAT FORMULA . . . TRY IT AND ENJOY THE
   JOB OF LIFE. PLANT THE SEED AND IT WILL GROW.
3. HUNTING FOR BETTER SPENDS ENERGY THAT IS
   BETTER SPENT HUNTING HAPPINESS IN WHAT YOU
   HAVE. ENJOY AND BE HAPPY NOW.

WEEK NINE—the giving diet

Monday	walk a mile in your shoes
Tuesday	ride a bike for a mile any style
Wednesday	lift your own weight in total resistance, 2 times
Thursday	do sit-ups/crunches for the size of your waist, 3 times
Friday	do push ups for the age of your car 5 times
Saturday	walk up stairs for the size of your shoes, 4 times
Sunday	take a respite . . . each day meditate for the time it takes to

go to sleep then recite your best affirmative image. Give of yourself to others
and find joy in their happiness. A total of 1,400 calories burned this week.

CHAPTER TEN

Stress Free Aging

(Stop cynical complaining about politics, religion, sex, taxes, money and social obstacles to your success, start using this book to find your role and acceptance of these situations and put them in perspective for your stress free life by being a part of the solutions).

I CATCH MY self these days complaining about everything that seems outside of my circle of influence (as demonstrated by my frustration with oppressive government voiced before this chapter) . . . maybe I am assuming I am perfect and no one else is . . . what a flawed approach to life. I am working on being more receptive to what appears to be stupid and is really another point of view that I do not agree with.

If I accomplish this learning curve I will have much less stress in my life and more receptive listeners to my life style opinions.

Yes there is much to complain about . . . negative influences put you in a negative frame of mind if you let it . . . I am stopping that as of now. And so can you . . . think better, live longer, happier, healthier more prosperous lives.

Stress . . . the act of letting things get to you. De-Stressors . . . the act of avoiding or counteracting things that get to you.

- Aches and pains . . . exercise until you avoid them
- Worries and concerns . . . counteract them with thoughts of joy, happiness and hope
- Financial and economic threats . . . think about solutions not the problems . . . and the how will emerge from your creative mind . . .

creative thinking is spurred by physical and mental exercise more than any other act

- Personal tragedies and emotional depression . . . get the mind and body working for a common cause either in exercise or in work related activities
- Getting old before your time . . . if you have abused your mind and body for years a reversal will take some stress relievers every day . . . better activities of daily living (diet, exercise, meditation and hopefulness) . . . if you are not able to do this you have given into the inevitable health and aging issues . . . stop them now and forever be grateful that you did.

The results are guaranteed:

1. You will be happier
2. You will be healthier
3. You will feel younger
4. You will not age due to stress

The beneficiaries will be:

1. Family
2. Business associates
3. Relatives
4. Friends
5. Yourself

STOP
START
SIGN

CHAPTER TEN EXERCISE Stop cynical complaining (about politics, religion, sex, taxes, money and social obstacles to your success) . . . START: daily affirmations about yourself for your self value. HERE IS THE OPPORTUNITY . . .

STOP COMPLAINING ABOUT SEX, POLITICS, RELIGION, TAXES, LACK OF MONEY AND SUCCESS . . . HOW CAN WE GET PASSED WHAT WE TERM REALITY . . . JUST MAKE BELIEVE THAT YOU ARE NOT GOING TO STRESS ABOUT THE THINGS YOU CANNOT CHANGE . . . BUT CHANGE WHAT YOU CAN AND BE HAPPY.

1) FROM NOW ON BE HAPPY, HEALTHY AND PROSPEROUS AND STRESS WILL BE IN YOUR REAR VIEW MIRROR.
2) YOU ARE NEVER TOO OLD TO LIVE AND ARE ALWAYS TOO YOUNG TO DIE SO LIVE BIG AND PUT WORRY, HATE, STRESS AND CIRCUMTANCE IN THE HANDS OF THE TOO OLD TO GROW AND CHANGE CROWD.

WEEK TEN YOU ARE THE WINNER—with 1,400 calories burned each week. On each day you willed your way to self-healthy habits as

Mondays	you have walked a total of 10 miles in your shoes
Tuesdays	you have ridden your bike a total of 10 miles any style
Wednesdays	you have lifted your own weight 2 times total resistance, 20 times

Thursdays   you've done 100's of sit-ups/crunches losing waist
Fridays   you've done 100's of push ups for your age and mind
Saturdays   you have walked up stairs for the size of your shoes, 40 times
Sundays   you have taken time for your self. Finding that living is an
option, dying is not, but when is. A total of 14,000 calories spent in 10
weeks . . . to be in control of when life ends by practicing self-health.

Congratulations on completing the 10 week journey to better habits,
to better health, to better hope, to a longer life. Now, in the next 10 weeks,
you can practice what we all preach . . . "I want to lose weight, have a
happy marriage, be satisfied with my job, have more money and not have
to win Mega Millions lotto to do it".

STARTSMART & FINISH STRONG

PLAN YOUR EPITAPH
NEVER TOO OLD TO LIVE
NEVER TOO LATE TO CHANGE

ALWAYS THINK FOREVER YOUNG

Who said "only time will tell" . . . is time running out on you to stop uncontrolled aging? All of us are aging at our own rate. You can choose to defer the process by using the methods proposed in this book . . . but that does not insure the avoidance of infections, falls, complications from the ER and diseases caught from others. The only way to avoid that is to stay out of places that breed such things:

- Hospitals
- Doctor's offices
- Nursing homes
- Emergency rooms
- Outpatient clinics

- Unsanitary businesses
- Your own unsanitary practices and depressive thoughts
- Compulsive and destructive behaviors

What is a reasonable age to work towards . . . the experts say the body of work that we have inherited should last 120 years if properly maintained . . . average life expectancy currently is 78 for both sexes. Wow! What a difference another 42 years could make on your social security check . . . while some of us will have the opportunity to live beyond a century most of the boomers will not . . . hopefully then, it will be of a quality that warrants the effort it takes to at least get to 100.

Those I have been around who are unhealthy cannot imagine suffering until the century mark . . . that is the point of this book . . . being 100 is because you want to live well because you are well. Wellness is the bridge to eternity.

Signs and symptoms of true eternal youth:

- Happy
- Healthy
- Prosperous
- Faithful
- Positive
- Goal Seeking

What's your emotional and mental biological age? More or less than your chronological age . . . Dr. Rubin and Dr. Oz have a calculator that will tell you. Log onto *www.RealAge.com* and calculate your biological age . . . then compare it to your chronological age. Do you seek a comfortable nest egg or fill your empty nest with work, hope and enterprise? We all should strive for this purpose to survive as a society.

Mind Exercise one: make an affirmation that "I can and will change my living habits. If you are emotionally old . . . the sun is setting on your future. No hope, no job, no marriage, no relationships, no life . . . If you are mentally old, the moon has eclipsed on your past, no dreams fulfilled, no love gained, no successful events, no joyful memories, no happy bed time stories, no value of life as you know it. Simply, it is from stinkin' thinkin' so get control of your mind.

Mind Exercise two: make a confirmation that "I will seek and find the good life happily and healthy". This state of affairs can and must be attained for you to age naturally and happy and healthy, and prosperous. Many will just accept unhappiness as happenstance that one must endure, while in waiting for happenstance to change. Guess what, it does not happen if your stance is on blaming others or just good ole circumstance. Good luck on making that work.

Mind Exercise three: find the destination you want "it is my destiny to be happy, healthy and prosperous beyond my natural years". To get there the journey to cure your doubt is, as always, in your head . . . you either think young or feel old . . . why not feel young and forget thinkin' old.

Exercise four: write your Epitaph with new habits and be "never too old to live" and "never too young to change" using the following human examples of overcoming human inadequacies to attain greatness and become an icon of the ages. The following are examples of achievement cut short by circumstances not stress free aging. Think as they lived and age stress free as you live.

ABRAHAM LINCOLN—unattractive, but articulate and brave beyond his short life . . . died early but lives on in infamy

MARTIN LUTHER KING—the rainbow visionary who died tragically following his dream for all of us

WINSTON CHURCHILL—fat and somewhat sloppy, but a great leader and orator . . . died early but lives on in infamy

FRANKLIN ROOSEVELT—polio victim, but able to overcome adversity through his power of the spoken words . . . died early but lives on in infamy

JOHN AND ROBERT KENNEDY—a product of their Father's passion for leadership . . . both died tragically but live on in our hearts

RONALD REGAN—a common man, but intelligent in a common sense way . . . his mind died early

BABE RUTH—pudgy and an alcoholic, but had short steps to a big time game . . . died early but lives on in infamy

GEORGE HALAS—grumpy old man, but director of men . . . died early but lives on in infamy

GEORGE WASHINGTON—stood for Self-Health, but fought for his country . . . died early but lives on in infamy

THOMAS JEFFERSON—too smart for his own good, but had logic down pat . . . died early but lives on in infamy

CASEY STENGAL—old timer, but never too old to win . . . died his way and lives on in infamy

RED ARBACH—no bigger than his cigars, but bigger than his opposition . . . died his way and lives on in infamy

JESSIE OWENS—out ran his race, but he caught the eye of all of the World with Worldly results . . . died early but lives on in infamy

JOHN WOODEN—he could inspire all ages with his words, but never brought attention to himself . . . died in his own way and lives on in infamy

JACKIE RONINSON—he was put on earth to bring down discrimination, but he brought down the house in doing so . . . died early but lives on in infamy

"The point is, they lived their way into our hearts, by believing they could make a difference and so can you."

FOR THE FINAL EXERCISE PLEASE GO TO YOUR "LAST WILL TO LIVE TESTAMENT" ON THE NEXT PAGE AND MAKE YOUR LIFE'S COMMITMENT TO BE WHAT YOU ARE MEANT TO BE. I CALL THIS **STAGING** YOUR LIFE . . . WE STAGE WHAT WE GET:

S elf is my destiny

T ime is my ally

AGING is my plan

FOR A BETTER LIFE ON THE STAGE OF FOREVER.

MY LAST "WILL TO LIVE" TESTAMENT

MY NAME: _____

MY BIOLOGICAL BIRTH DATE: _____

MY CHRONILOGICAL BIRTH DATE: _____

CALCULATE YOUR CURRENT BIOLOGICAL AGE: _____ IF THIS IS MORE THAN YOUR CHRONILOGICAL AGE YOU WILL DIE YOUNGER THAN YOU SHOULD.

MY LAST WILL IN TESTAMENT IS TO LIVE LONGER. TO DO SO I,

	YES	NO
WILL STOP		
1. Negative thinking,	_____	_____
2. Eating for desire,	_____	_____
3. Being inactive,	_____	_____
4. Hating my life,	_____	_____
5. Finding fault of everything,	_____	_____
6. Being angry,	_____	_____
7. Destructive habits,	_____	_____
8. Hunting a better spouse,	_____	_____
9. Hunting a better job	_____	_____
10. Forming judgmental opinions	_____	_____

	YES	NO

WILL START

		YES	NO
1.	Positive thinking,	_____	_____
2.	Eating for hunger,	_____	_____
3.	Being active,	_____	_____
4.	Loving my life,	_____	_____
5.	Finding good in everything,	_____	_____
6.	Being happy,	_____	_____
7.	Pursuing good habits,	_____	_____
8.	Accepting my spouse as my soul mate,	_____	_____
9.	Accepting my job or get a new one,	_____	_____
10.	Forming hopeful thoughts.	_____	_____

MY WILL TO LIVE AGE GOAL _____

SIGNED BY: _____

DATED: _____

START NOW

MY SELF-HEALTH PLAN:

I WILL START   <u>START DATE</u>

1. Being positive   _____
2. Eating for health   _____
3. Loving my future   _____
4. Finding the good in life   _____
5. Finding good in myself   _____
6. Finding good in others   _____
7. Finding good habits   _____
8. Enjoying my spouse   _____
9. Enjoying my job   _____
10. Giving of myself for a better life _____

MY LAST "WILL TO LIVE" TESTAMENT STARTS WITH MY "WILL TO LIVE AGELESS" TODAY.

I HAVE DECIDED THAT I CAN LIVE A LONGER, BETTER LIFE IF I INTEND TO AND ATTEND TO MY PLAN. AND THEN I CAN PLAN MY EPITAPH AS FOLLOWS:

IN "MY LAST WILL TO LIVE TESTAMENT" I PLAN TO LEAVE THIS LIFE FEELING FULFILLED AND HAPPY EVERY DAY FROM NOW ON.

DATE OF MY EXPECTED DEPARTURE:_____

SIGNED: _____

SWORN AND ATTESTED TO BY: _____

NEVER
TOO OLD

TOO LIVE

LIFE EXPECTANCY TABLE

YEAR	MALE	FEMALE
1900	40	45
1925	50	55
1950	55	60
1975	60	65
2000	76	82

| 2010 | 77 | 81 |
| 2025 (estimates) | 73 | 75 |

Why would life expectance take a down turn?

1. Obesity
2. Incurable cancers
3. Exacerbated diabetes
4. Respiratory failure
5. Untreatable infections
6. Strokes
7. Falls and
8. Complications of inactivity
9. Chemical dependencies
10. No preventive measures
11. No health preservation measures

Our society does not move the body or the brain enough . . . and we take life for granted while taking pills, enchanted with modern medicine . . . which are likely creating chronic conditions not curing our own bad habits.

Computers, autos, escalators, elevators, moving walkways, buses, trains, planes, all are making it too easy to DIE YOUNGER AND HARDER TO LIVE LONGER.

MIND DIVIDED BY TIME + MOVEMENT X WEIGHT = AGING AND QUALITY OF LIFE

THIS IS THE E=MC2 OF AGING . . . A BODY IN MOTION WILL STAY IN MOTION UNTIL THE MIND SHUTS DOWN THE ENERGY IT TAKES TO MATTER.

ACCESS *www.nevertooooldtolive.com* THE RHOADS DOWNSIZER CALCULATOR USABLE WITH EXCEL 7.0

"SELF-HEALTH"
STAGING GOALS:
- *FUN FOR THE MIND*
- *LOVE FOR THE HEART*
- *HAPPINESS FOREVER*

NEVER TOO OLD
TO BE HEALTHY

SELF-HEALTH FOUND

You are now determining your life time, weight, happiness, longevity . . . and you can out run that car . . . so the practice of Self-Health is now you; self is the body, mind & soul creating health:

S cience

E ngineered

L ife

F ulfillment

H ow you're thinking controls your prosperity

E ating when you are hungry and full keeps you thin

A ge only measures your increased longevity

L ife is showing others your stage and performance

T ime is now enhanced by the way you use of it

H ealth is your journey not a dreaded destination, (learn to love it and

you shall be loved and healthy)

HI HANDSOME . . . MY NAME IS ROSE

(Author unknown)

The first day of school our professor introduced himself and challenged us to get to know someone we didn't already know. I stood up to look around when a gentle hand touched my shoulder. I turned around to find a wrinkled, little old lady beaming up at me with a smile that lit up her entire being. She said, 'Hi handsome. My name is Rose. I'm eighty-seven years old. Can I give you a hug?' I laughed and enthusiastically responded; 'Of course you may!' and she gave me a giant squeeze. Why are you in college at such a young, innocent age?' I asked. She jokingly replied, 'I'm here to meet a rich husband, get married, and have a couple of kids . . . ' 'No seriously,' I asked. I was curious what may have motivated her to be taking on this challenge at her age.

'I always dreamed of having a college education and now I'm getting one!' she told me. After class we walked to the student union building and shared a chocolate milkshake. We became instant friends. Every day for the next three months we would leave class together and talk nonstop. I was always mesmerized listening to this 'time machine' as she shared her wisdom and experience with me. Over the course of the year, Rose became a campus icon and she easily made friends wherever she went. She loved to dress up and she reveled in the attention bestowed upon her from the other students. She was living it up. At the end of the semester we invited Rose to speak at our football banquet. I'll never forget what she taught us. She was introduced and stepped up to the podium. As she began to deliver her prepared speech, she dropped her three by five cards on the floor.

Frustrated and a little embarrassed she leaned into the microphone and simply said, 'I'm sorry I'm so jittery. I gave up beer for Lent and this whiskey is killing me! I'll never get my speech back in order so let me just tell you what I know.' As we laughed she cleared her throat and began, 'We do not stop playing because we are old; we grow old because we stop playing. There are only four secrets to staying young, being happy, and achieving success. You have to laugh and find humor every day. You've got to have a dream. When you lose your dreams, you die. We have so many people walking around who are dead and don't even know it! Where is a huge difference between growing older and growing up. If you are nineteen years old and lie in bed for one full year and don't do one productive thing, you will turn twenty years old. If I am eighty-seven years old and stay in bed for a year and never do anything I will turn eighty-eight. Anybody! Can grow older. That doesn't take any talent or ability. The idea is to grow up by always finding opportunity in change. Have no regrets.

The elderly usually don't have regrets for what we did, but rather for things we did not do. The only people who fear death are those with regrets. 'She concluded her speech by courageously singing 'The Rose.' She challenged each of us to study the lyrics and live them out in our daily lives. At the year's end Rose finished the college degree she had begun all those months ago.

One week after graduation Rose died peacefully in her sleep. Over two thousand college students attended her funeral in tribute to the wonderful woman who taught by example that it's never too late to be all you can possibly be. These words have been passed along in loving memory of ROSE. REMEMBER, GROWING OLDER IS MANDATORY. GROWING UP IS OPTIONAL. We make a Living by what we get. We make a Life by what we give.

JERRY RHOADS

AGE STRONG (like the Rose)

Body = strength = pink rose
Mind = hope = yellow rose
Soul = peace = white rose
Heart = love = red rose

All along
We thought wrong
Talk of getting old
Sad stories untold

While we worry on
Our sun wanes at dawn
Losing sleep
With no dreams we keep

(continued)

Awaken child of time
Hoping to stay young is no crime
For it is the strength of will
That takes time to kill

Pages are written long and hard
About mind decline and discard
But sages state the truth
We all have eternal youth

Find it in your soul
To set life's true goal
That growing young is in our reach
If we practice what we preach

Avoid the wrong . . . so we can Finish Strong

By: Jerry L. Rhoads